Sunny
and
Rainy

PAGE PUBLISHING, INC.
Conneaut Lake, PA

First originally published by Page Publishing 2020

ISBN 978-1-64628-308-8 (pbk)
ISBN 978-1-6624-2643-8 (hc)
ISBN 978-1-64628-309-5 (digital)

Printed in the United States of America

Sunny
and
Rainy

LISA W BRYANT

To Mother Nature, two children were born: one was bright and chummy. She took one look and said out loud, "I think I'll call him Sunny."

3

The other child was a little girl, serious yet brainy. Mother Nature looked at her and said, "I'll name her Rainy."

Sunny and Rainy grew up happily; their differences never kept them apart. Mother Nature taught them well, with lots of love right from the start.

When old enough, Mother Nature sat them down for a long talk. Concerning their gifts, their reasons for being, and the special paths on which they would walk.

"Sunny, oh, Sunny, you are so funny. You are beaming, bubbly, and bright. Many people near and far will be warmed by the kiss of your light. You will be the largest star in the universe. You will be number

one. Affectionately, most will refer to you as a ball of gas called The Sun. You will feed all of the plants, flowers and trees bathing them with your glow. Surrounding them with heat and love, helping them to grow."

Rainy excitedly stated, "Wow, Mommy! That sounds great! May I be a sun too?"

"No, dear Rainy, you will have another job to do. Oh, Rainy, my sweetheart, what a precious gift you are. You will be just as important as the world's biggest star. Your wonderful presence will fill the world with oceans, rivers, and streams. You will clean the bodies and satisfy

the thirst of every living being. You shall wash buildings, bridges, and streets with purpose and with power. All of the plants, flowers, and trees will grow tall from the quench of your shower.

"The inner self of human beings will be affected too. They will be taught valuable lessons through the both of you.

Sunny will shine through the spirit of humans that a smiling face will project. Rainy's water will provide the tears giving chance for their souls to reflect.

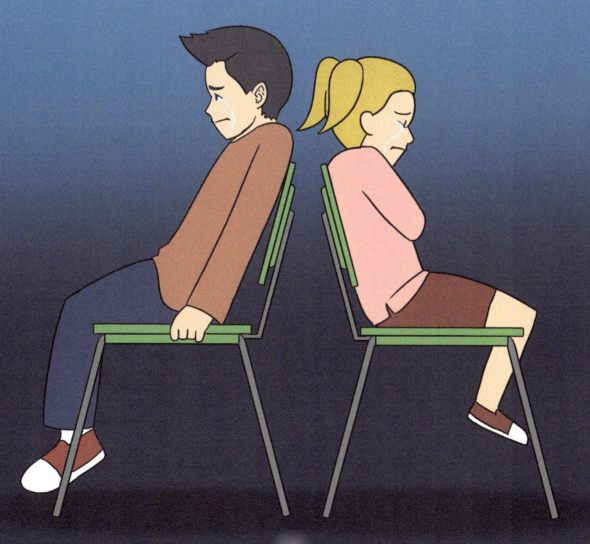

"So there, my children, go forth and fulfill your duties. Shine, Warm, Cleanse, Quench all the while creating beauty.

"Your lives will be long lasting and your message, simple and plain. Everything grows stronger with a little sunshine and rain."

About the Author

Lisa W Bryant writes poetry and short stories. Since childhood, she has had a wonderful relationship with reading. Her family didn't have a lot growing up, but they always had books. It is fascinating to her to explore other people's truths and imaginations through the pages of a book. Therefore, she is honored to share a bit of hers with her readers. Her professional background is in nursing. She worked as an LPN (licensed practical nurse) in hospitals and nursing homes for many years. She has two children: DeVaughn and Brittney. The love of her life is her granddaughter, Aleena Rose. She has lived her whole life in Pittsburgh, Pennsylvania. She thanks the Lord Jesus for being with her every step of the way in every part of her life.

CPSIA information can be obtained
at www.ICGtesting.com
Printed in the USA
LVHW070335211020
669279LV00008B/355

9 781646 283088